HEROIC JOBS

FIGHTING CRIME

Ellen Labrecque

Raintree

Chicago, Illinois

www.capstonepub.com
Visit our website to find out more information about Heinemann-Raintree books.

To order:
☎ Phone 888-454-2279
🖥 Visit www.capstonepub.com
to browse our catalog and order online.

Edited by Dan Nunn, Rebecca Rissman, and Catherine Veitch
Designed by Joanne Malivoire
Picture research by Elizabeth Alexander
Originated by Capstone Global Library
Printed and bound in China by CTPS

15 14 13 12 11
10 9 8 7 6 5 4 3 2 1

Library of Congress Cataloging-in-Publication Data
Labrecque, Ellen.
  Fighting crime / Ellen Labrecque.
    p. cm.—(Heroic jobs)
  Includes bibliographical references and index.
  ISBN 978-1-4109-4355-2 (hb)—ISBN 978-1-4109-4362-0 (pb) 1. Police—Juvenile literature. 2. Police—Special weapons and tactics units—Juvenile literature. 3. Raids (Military science)—Juvenile literature. I. Title.
  HV7922.L23 2012
  363.2'32—dc22   2011015810

Acknowledgments
We would like to thank the following for permission to reproduce photographs: © Newspix / News Ltd / 3rd Party Managed Reproduction & Supply Rights p. 20 (James Elsby); Alamy pp. 5 (© Les Gibbon), 6 (© Les Gibbon), 14 (© Altered Images), 16 (© Michael Matthews - Police Images), 17 (© Les Gibbon), 19 (© Jeff Greenberg), 22 (© Michael Matthews – Police Images), 26 (© JHB Photography); Corbis pp.11 (© Image Source), 18 (© Miguel Fernandes/epa), 21 (© Enrique Marcarian/Reuters), 24 (© Ed Kashi), 25 (© Stephanie Sinclair/VII); Getty Images pp. 4 (Attila Kisbenedek/AFP), 7 (Metropolitan Police), 9 (Chris Jackson), 10 (FRANCOIS LO PRESTI/AFP), 12 (Nicholas Maeterlinck/AFP), 15 (EVARISTO SA/AFP); iStockphoto p. 28 (© Terraxplorer); Photolibrary pp. 8 (Jochen Tack), 13 (moodboard), 27 (Alain Le Bot/Photononstop); Rex Features pp. 23 (Nils Jorgensen), 29 Daniel Graves.

Cover photograph of police cars in action reproduced with permission of Photolibrary (Jochen Tack/Imagebroker.net).

Every effort has been made to contact copyright holders of material reproduced in this book. Any omissions will be rectified in subsequent printings if notice is given to the publisher.

Some words are shown in bold, **like this**. You can find out what they mean by looking in the glossary.

Contents

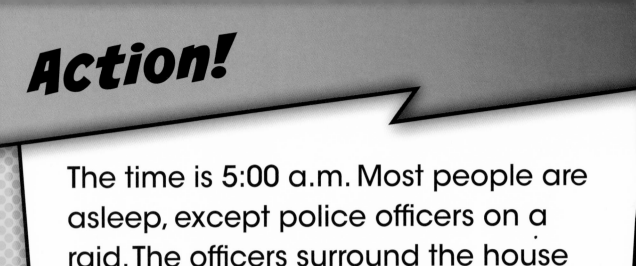

Action!

The time is 5:00 a.m. Most people are asleep, except police officers on a raid. The officers surround the house of a suspected criminal. They knock loudly on the door and shout to be let in. When nobody answers, the officers break the door down and charge in.

What Is a Police Raid?

A police raid is when police officers surprise **suspects** and **arrest** them, or search for **evidence**. Suspects are people that the police think are guilty of a crime. Raids are used when police think the suspects will **resist**, or fight against, the arrest.

Did you know?
Police raids that take place in the early morning are also called "dawn raids."

7

Who Are the Police?

Police officers are in charge of keeping order in their local area. Officers stop, or **prevent**, crime from happening. They also discover, or **detect**, crime. They must be smart and honest. They must also be very fit.

Police officers also
need to be brave.

The Investigation

Police **investigate**, or research facts about a crime, before making a raid. During an investigation, police officers collect **evidence** to prove what has happened. They also **interrogate** people who may have seen what happened. These people are called **witnesses**.

11

Teamwork Works

Each member of the police raid team has a job. Some officers look for **evidence** at the scene of the crime. Other officers are **lookouts**. Lookouts watch to make sure the **suspect** doesn't escape. They also keep people away from the crime scene.

Dogs are part of the team, too!

Danger!

Raids can be dangerous. Police never know for certain what they will find. There could be more **suspects** than they first thought. There could also be explosives, such as bombs, or loaded guns. The more prepared the police are, the safer they will be.

All of these weapons were seized in a police raid in November 2010, in Rio de Janeiro, Brazil.

Equipment

Each police officer wears about 35 pounds of equipment on a raid. The equipment includes a bulletproof vest to protect against getting hurt, firearms, a radio, and handcuffs to **arrest** the **suspects**.

handcuffs

Did you know?
A police officer may use a taser gun to fire an electric shock at a suspect if the suspect is threatening the officer with violence. Usually, a taser gun does no long-term harm.

17

Catching Drug Dealers

Drug dealers are criminals who sell drugs **illegally**. These drugs can make the people who take them very ill or even kill them. The police try to stop people from selling drugs illegally.

These police officers are seizing illegal drugs after a drugs raid in Brazil.

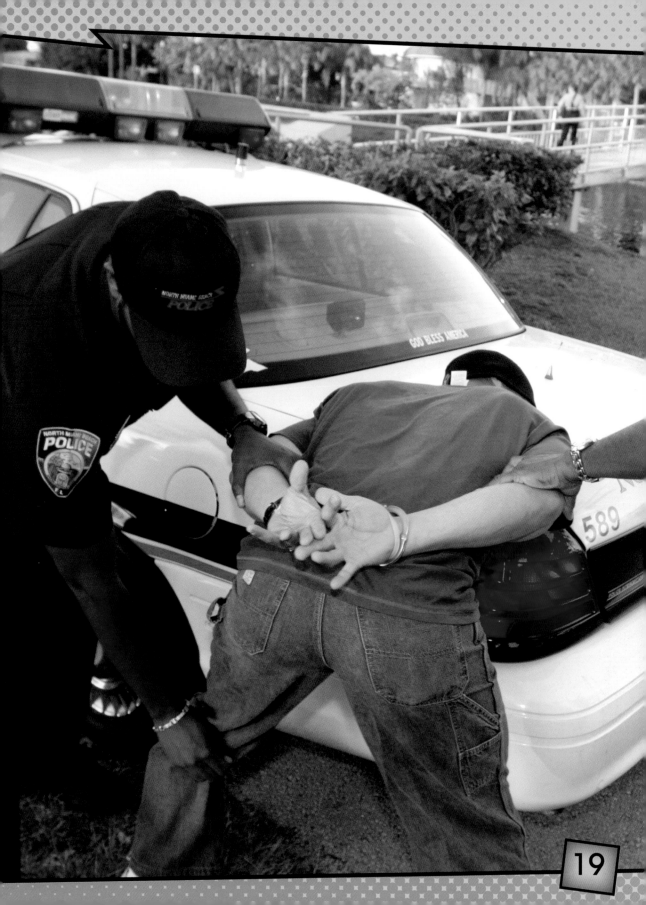

Stolen Goods

Some police raids are to recover stolen goods. In a raid near Sydney, Australia, in January 2009, police discovered the country's biggest shoplifting crime ever. A large warehouse was filled with stolen makeup, perfumes, razor blades, and shampoos. The total value of the **loot** was millions of dollars.

Escape!

Sometimes, a suspected criminal escapes in a car during a police raid. The police drive after the suspect. Police helicopters also fly above the cars. They tell the officers in the police cars which way the **suspect** is driving.

Caught in the Act

Sometimes, the police will get some secret information, or a **tip-off**, to tell them that a crime is going to take place. They set up **surveillance**, or keep watch, at the place where the suspected crime is supposed to happen. Then, they can catch the criminals red-handed!

Becoming a Police Officer

You need to be brave to become a police officer. You will need to train at a police training center, as well as pass written and spoken tests. Police officers should be smart and fit. They are the world's real superheroes. They are crime fighters!

Stay Safe

In an emergency, call for help. It is important to give as much information about the emergency as possible. Never ever make **hoax** 911 calls. It could cost lives. When someone has called 911, emergency help will soon be at the scene.

Did you know?
There are different emergency telephone numbers around the world:
- United States: 911
- Australia: 000
- most of Europe: 112
- UK: 999

Glossary

arrest catch someone and charge them with a crime

detect discover or catch

evidence something found that can prove or disprove that a crime took place

hoax trick, where someone says something has happened, but they are not telling the truth

illegally do something that is against the law

interrogate ask questions in a serious manner

investigate try to find out the truth about something

lookout person who watches for danger

loot stolen goods or money

prevent stop from happening

resist try to stop something from happening

surveillance watch kept over a person

suspect someone who is thought to have done something wrong

tip-off piece of private or secret information

witness somone who sees an event, such as a crime, happening and can tell other people about it

Find Out More

Books

Enz, Tammy. *Beyond the Bars: Exploring the Secrets of a Police Station*. Mankato, Minn.: Capstone Press, 2010.

Miller, Connie Colwell. *SWAT Teams: Armed and Ready*. Mankato, Minn.: Capstone Press, 2008.

Watson, Stephanie. *A Career as a Police Officer*. New York: Rosen Classroom, 2010.

Websites

www.billtheburglar.org
This website has tips on ways to secure your home against burglars.

www.bls.gov/k12/law01.htm
This website has lots of information about what it's like to work as a police officer.

www.police.vic.gov.au/content.asp?Document_ID=12260
This website about a police force in Australia is packed with interesting facts about the police and fun activities.

Index